AF225743

# Accounting for Retirement Benefits

Steven M. Bragg

Copyright © 2025 by AccountingTools, Inc. All rights reserved.

Published by AccountingTools, Inc., Centennial, Colorado.

No part of this publication may be reproduced, stored in a retrieval system, or transmitted in any form or by any means, except as permitted under Section 107 or 108 of the 1976 United States Copyright Act, without the prior written permission of the Publisher. Requests to the Publisher for permission should be addressed to Steven M. Bragg, 6727 E. Fremont Place, Centennial, CO 80112.

Limit of Liability/Disclaimer of Warranty: While the publisher and author have used their best efforts in preparing this book, they make no representations or warranties with respect to the accuracy or completeness of the contents of this book and specifically disclaim any implied warranties of merchantability or fitness for a particular purpose. No warranty may be created or extended by written sales materials. The advice and strategies contained herein may not be suitable for your situation. You should consult with a professional where appropriate. Neither the publisher nor author shall be liable for any loss of profit or any other commercial damages, including but not limited to special, incidental, consequential, or other damages.

ISBN 978-1-64221-269-3

For more information about AccountingTools® products, visit our Web site at www.accountingtools.com.

# Table of Contents

# About the Author

**Steven Bragg, CPA,** has been the chief financial officer or controller of four companies, as well as a consulting manager at Ernst & Young. He received a master's degree in finance from Bentley College, an MBA from Babson College, and a Bachelor's degree in Economics from the University of Maine. He has been a two-time president of the Colorado Mountain Club, and is an avid alpine skier, mountain biker, and certified master diver. Mr. Bragg resides in Centennial, Colorado. He has written more than 300 books and courses, including *New Controller Guidebook, GAAP Guidebook,* and *Payroll Management*. He has also written the science fiction novel *Under an Autumn Sun*, first book in *The Auditors* trilogy.

Steven maintains the accountingtools.com web site, which contains continuing professional education courses, the Accounting Best Practices podcast, and thousands of articles on accounting subjects.

## Buy Additional AccountingTools Courses

AccountingTools offers more than 1,500 hours of CPE courses, with concentrations in accounting, auditing, finance, taxation, and ethics. Related courses that you might like include:

- Essentials of Employment Law
- How to Audit Benefit and Compensation Plans
- How to Audit Payroll
- Human Resources Guidebook
- Payroll Management

Go to accountingtools.com/cpe to view these additional courses.

# Accounting for Retirement Benefits

## Introduction

Many organizations offer benefit plans that provide income to retired personnel in exchange for services provided. Of these plans, the bulk of the funds are concentrated in pension plans; a pension plan is a pool of funds to which contributions are made by an employer, which are then made available to employees upon their retirement.

This manual addresses the accounting for two types of pension plans, called defined benefit plans and defined contribution plans, detailing the accounting required by the employer. Nearly all of the discussion is concentrated on defined benefit plans, which require ongoing estimations of and accounting for future costs that may be incurred, as well as changes to existing benefits.

Some of the complexity of this topic is caused by a rare circumstance in GAAP – where provisions are made to allow a business to defer costs and recognize them in later periods through amortization. This approach contravenes the vastly more common approach of charging all costs to expense as incurred. While this type of modified accounting undoubtedly allows a business to defer expense recognition, it causes ongoing headaches for accountants, and likely increases the profits of the actuarial industry.

The guidance in this manual applies to all entities.

## Overview of Retirement Benefits

A retirement benefit is one in which the employer promises to deliver a fixed benefit to its employees at some point in the future. Examples of these benefits are pensions and health benefits to be paid following the retirement of employees. Employees qualify for retirement benefits either through the passage of time, by attaining a certain age, or a combination of both. Retirement benefits paid to employees may begin as soon as they retire, or the benefits may be delayed until a certain age is reached, or even when employees elect to begin accepting benefits.

The underlying principle that drives the accounting for retirement benefits is that the employer only provides these benefits in exchange for the ongoing services of employees, which makes the benefits a form of deferred compensation, where the employer incurs an obligation for the compensation as services are rendered by employees. Consequently, the employer must estimate the amount of future expenditure that will be made and recognize a portion of it in the current period. Expense recognition occurs before the benefits are paid, because employees are earning these future benefits via their services in earlier periods.

It is possible that the service costs associated with retirement benefits will be capitalized into inventory as part of the application of factory overhead to inventory. These costs can also be capitalized into fixed assets, if they relate to employee labor in constructing fixed assets.

## Defined Benefit Plans

In a defined benefit retirement plan, the employer provides a pre-determined periodic payment to employees after they retire. For example, an employer might promise to pay an inflation-adjusted monthly amount of $1,000 to an employee following her retirement, and continuing for the rest of her life. The amount of this future payment depends upon a number of future events, such as estimates of employee lifespan, how long current employees will continue to work for the company, and the pay level of employees just prior to their retirement. As long as the plan continues to operate, the employer is responsible for the payment of the defined benefits; if the amount of money in the pension fund is not sufficient to pay for expected benefits, then the employer must pay in the amount of the expected shortfall. These additional payments may continue through the life of the plan.

In essence, the accounting for defined benefit plans revolves around the estimation of the future payments to be made, and recognizing the related expense in the periods in which employees are rendering the services that qualify them to receive payments in the future under the terms of the plan. Actuaries are used to derive the estimated amounts of future payments based on (for example) mortality rates, expected employee turnover, expected interest income, future salaries, and the early retirement of employees. The accountant then uses these estimates to generate accounting entries.

There are a number of costs associated with defined benefit plans that may at first appear arcane. The following table contains a summary of the relevant costs, which sum to the net periodic pension cost that is recognized in each accounting period.

### Cost Components in a Defined Benefit Plan

| Cost | Explanation |
|---|---|
| + Service cost | This is the actuarial present value of benefits related to services rendered during the current reporting period. The cost includes an estimate of the future compensation levels of employees from which benefit payments will be derived. |
| + Interest cost | This is the interest on the projected benefit obligation. It accrues each year on the projected benefit obligation, which was originally recorded on a discounted basis. Interest cost is a financial item, rather than a cost related to employee compensation. The actuary assists in the selection of the interest rate to be used to discount the projected benefit obligation.[1] |

---

[1] The interest rate used should reflect the rate at which the employer can settle its pension benefits. Thus, an employer should look for rates of return on high-quality fixed income investments that are currently available, and which have cash flows that approximately match the timing and amount of the anticipated benefit payouts.

| + Actual return on plan assets | This is the difference between the fair values of beginning and ending plan assets, adjusted for contributions and benefit payments. The return on assets is derived from interest and dividends accumulating within the pension plan, as well as from changes in the fair value of the plan's assets. It is a financial item, rather than a cost related to employee compensation. |
|---|---|
| + Amortization of prior service costs | When an employer issues a plan amendment, it may contain increases in benefits that are based on services rendered by employees in prior periods. If so, the cost of these additional benefits is amortized over the future periods in which those employees active on the amendment date are expected to receive benefits. |
| + Gain or loss | This is the gain or loss resulting from a change in the value of a projected benefit obligation from changes in assumptions, or changes in the value of plan assets. |
| = Net periodic pension cost | |

One of the components of a defined benefit plan that was included in the preceding table was the actual return on plan assets. This return is calculated by computing the change in plan assets during the measurement period, and then adding contributions made to the plan during the period and subtracting out any benefits paid. Thus, the calculation is:

$$\textbf{Actual Return} = (\text{Plan assets ending balance} - \text{Plan assets beginning balance}) - (\text{Contributions} + \text{Benefits paid})$$

If the actual return on plan assets is positive, the return is subtracted from the calculation of pension expense. If the actual return is negative, the return is added to the calculation of pension expense.

---

**EXAMPLE**

The controller of Grissom Granaries calculates the actual return on the company's plan assets in the following manner:

| | | |
|---|---|---|
| Fair value of plan assets at end of period | | $10,000,000 |
| Less: fair value of plan assets at beginning of period | | 8,400,000 |
| Increase in fair value of plan assets | | 1,600,000 |
| Deduct: Contributions to plan during period | $1,000,000 | |
| Less: Benefits paid during period | 600,000 | - 400,000 |
| Actual return on plan assets | | $1,200,000 |

---

The accounting for the relevant defined benefit plan costs is as follows:

- *Service cost.* The amount of service cost recognized in earnings in each period is the incremental change in the actuarial present value of benefits related to services rendered during the current reporting period.
- *Interest cost.* The interest cost associated with the projected benefit obligation is recognized as incurred. This expense arises because the projected benefit obligation is initially recorded on a discounted basis; the obligation then accrues interest over the life of the employee.
- *Amortization of prior service costs.* These costs are charged to other comprehensive income on the date of the amendment, and then amortized to earnings over time. The amount to be amortized is derived by assigning an equal amount of expense to each future period of service for each employee who is expected to receive benefits. If most of the employees are inactive, the amortization period is instead the remaining life expectancy of the employees. Straight-line amortization of the cost over the average remaining service period is also acceptable. Once established, this amortization schedule is not usually revised, unless there is a plan curtailment or if events indicate that a shorter amortization period is warranted.

---

**EXAMPLE**

Armadillo Industries creates a pension plan amendment that grants $90,000 of prior service costs to the 200 employees in its Mississippi facility. The company expects the employees at this location to retire in accordance with the following schedule:

| Group | Number of Staff | Expected Year of Retirement |
|---|---|---|
| A | 20 | Year 1 |
| B | 40 | Year 2 |
| C | 80 | Year 3 |
| D | 40 | Year 4 |
| E | 20 | Year 5 |
| Total | 200 | |

The company uses the following grid to calculate the service years for each of the employee groups:

| | Service Years | | | | | |
|---|---|---|---|---|---|---|
| Year | Group A | Group B | Group C | Group D | Group E | Total |
| 1 | 20 | 40 | 80 | 40 | 20 | 200 |
| 2 | | 40 | 80 | 40 | 20 | 180 |
| 3 | | | 80 | 40 | 20 | 140 |
| 4 | | | | 40 | 20 | 60 |
| 5 | | | | | 20 | 20 |
| Totals | 20 | 80 | 240 | 160 | 100 | 600 |

There are 600 service years listed in the preceding table, over which the $90,000 prior service cost is to be allocated, which is $150 of cost per service year. Armadillo inserts the $150 per year figure into the following table to determine the amount of prior service cost amortization to recognize in each year.

| Year | Total of Service Years | × | Cost per Service Year | = | Amortization per Year |
|---|---|---|---|---|---|
| 1 | 200 | | $150 | | $30,000 |
| 2 | 180 | | 150 | | 27,000 |
| 3 | 140 | | 150 | | 21,000 |
| 4 | 60 | | 150 | | 9,000 |
| 5 | 20 | | 150 | | 3,000 |
| Totals | 600 | | | | $90,000 |

---

- *Prior service credits.* If a plan amendment reduces plan benefits, record it in other comprehensive income on the date of the amendment. This amount is then offset against any prior service cost remaining in accumulated other comprehensive income. Any residual amount of the credit is then amortized using the same methodology just noted for prior service costs.
- *Gains and losses.* Gains and losses can be recognized immediately if the method is applied consistently. If the election is not made to recognize them immediately, it is also possible to account for them as changes in other comprehensive income as they occur. If there is a gain or loss on the difference between the expected and actual amount of return on plan assets, recognize the difference in other comprehensive income in the period in which it occurs, and amortize it to earnings using the following calculation:
  1. Include the gain or loss in net pension cost for a year in which, as of the beginning of that year, the gain or loss is greater than 10% of the

> greater of the projected benefit obligation or the market-related value of plan assets.
>
> 2. If this test is positive, amortize the excess just noted over the average remaining service period of those active employees who are expected to receive benefits. If most of the plan participants are inactive, amortize the excess over their remaining life expectancy.

A key term that arises in the accounting for defined benefit plans is the *projected benefit obligation*. This is the actuarial present value of future benefits attributed to service already rendered by employees. The "actuarial" part of the definition refers to *expected* payments, since some payments will never be made, due to the turnover of employees before they vest, the death of employees who would otherwise have been entitled to payments, and so forth. The projected benefit obligation also incorporates assumptions regarding the future pay levels and service periods of existing employees, which tends to increase the amount of the benefit obligation in comparison to what the obligation would be based on current employee compensation levels and periods of service.

When a business incurs obligations for future pension payments, it should presumably begin accumulating assets into a pension plan that will be available to pay the pension benefits in the future. If the projected benefit obligation is greater than the fair value of the plan assets on the balance sheet date, the employer should recognize a liability for the difference (known as the *unfunded projected benefit obligation*). In those rare cases where plan assets exceed the projected benefit obligation, the employer recognizes an asset in the amount of the difference. If there are multiple plans, all overfunded plans should be aggregated for reporting purposes, and all underfunded plans should be aggregated for reporting purposes.

It is possible that the unfunded or overfunded projected benefit obligation will result in a temporary difference for income tax purposes. If so, recognize the deferred tax effects of the temporary difference within the year.

If there are adjustments to the funded status of a pension plan, net gains or losses, prior service costs, and so forth, the offset to these entries is other comprehensive income.

When the employer buys annuity contracts to cover the cost of future employee benefits, the cost of the benefits should be the same as the cost of acquiring the annuity contracts.

## Expense Attribution for Delayed Vesting

There are a number of methods available for assigning benefits to employees, usually with the intent of delaying the vesting of benefits. For example, a plan may provide no benefits after nine years of service, and then vests employees in a future benefit payment following the tenth year of service (known as *cliff vesting*). In these situations, do not defer the recognition of a benefit expense until the delayed vesting occurs. Instead, assume that the benefit accumulates over time in proportion to the number of completed periods of service, which means that there should be an ongoing accrual of the related benefit expense over time.

**EXAMPLE**

Uncanny Corporation has a defined benefit pension plan, under which it pays a pension benefit of $60 per month for the remainder of each employee's life for each year of service completed, up to a maximum of ten years of service. The actuary employed by Uncanny calculates that the average employee will have 210 months of life expectancy following their retirement from Uncanny, and will have the full 10 years of service completed as of their retirement. The actuarial present value discount is set at 0.35. Based on this information, the actuary calculates the following pension benefits attributable to each of Uncanny's employees:

| | |
|---|---:|
| Years of service period completed | 10 |
| × Pension benefit per month | × $60 |
| = Payment to be made per month to each employee | = $600 |
| × Average life expectancy (in months) | × 210 |
| = Gross pension payment | = $126,000 |
| × Actuarial present value discount rate | × 0.35 |
| = Present value of pension benefit | $44,100 |

## Discount Rates

Service costs are based on the actuarial present value of benefits to be paid in the future. A discount rate must be employed to arrive at this actuarial present value. The discount rate should be one that reflects the rate at which benefits can actually be settled. A good source of information for this discount rate is the rate implicit in the current prices of annuity contracts that an employer could purchase to settle a future benefit obligation. Another source of information is the rate of return on high-quality fixed income investments that are expected to be available through the period during which the pension benefits will be paid.

Interest rates vary, depending upon the time period of investments. Thus, the discount rate used for benefits to be paid to a group of 50-year old employees will likely be different from the discount rate used for benefits to be paid to a group of 30-year olds.

The discount rate(s) used will likely vary over time, which can have a profound impact on the amount of the employer's obligation, causing ongoing fluctuations in the amount of the reported pension liability.

## Settlements and Curtailments

A benefit plan may be adjusted or terminated at some point. Variations that may be encountered include:

- *Curtailments*. Employee services or the benefit plan itself may be terminated earlier than expected, which reduces or eliminates the accrual of additional benefits.

- *Settlements*. Lump-sum cash payments may be made to plan participants in exchange for their rights to receive pension benefits.

When benefit obligations are settled, curtailed, or terminated, net gains or losses and prior service costs are shifted from accumulated other comprehensive income to earnings. This transfer occurs in the period in which all pension obligations are settled, benefits are no longer accrued, no plan assets remain, employees are terminated, *and* the plan ceases to exist. Also, the plan cannot be replaced by another plan.

If only a portion of the projected benefit obligation is settled, recognize in earnings that portion of the settlement that represents the reduction in the projected benefit obligation.

If the cost of the settlements completed in a year is greater or less than the sum of the service and interest cost components of the net periodic pension cost for that period, record a gain or loss in the amount of the difference. If the cost is lower than the sum of the service and interest cost components, recognition in earnings is permitted, but not required. The manner in which management chooses to deal with a lower-cost situation should be followed consistently.

If an employer purchases an annuity contract in order to settle a benefit plan, and the annuity was purchased from an entity that the employer controls, settlement accounting cannot be used to record the transaction. Similarly, if the employer retains the risks and rewards associated with a benefit obligation, despite purchasing an annuity contract, settlement accounting cannot be used.

If there is a curtailment of a benefit plan, the associated amount of prior service cost already recorded in accumulated other comprehensive income that is related to future years of service should be recognized in earnings as a loss. Also, the projected benefit obligation may be increased or decreased by a curtailment. This is a curtailment gain in the amount by which it exceeds any loss included in accumulated other comprehensive income. This is a curtailment loss in the amount by which it exceeds any net gain included in accumulated other comprehensive income. A curtailment loss should be recognized in earnings when the amount can be reasonably estimated and the curtailment is probable. A curtailment gain should be recognized in earnings when the plan is formally suspended or the impacted employees are terminated.

---

**EXAMPLE**

Following the devastation of a major earthquake, Armadillo Industries closes down its California facility. The employees located there will no longer earn any benefits. As of the plan curtailment date, the actuarial assumptions associated with the plan are:

- Defined benefit obligation = $300,000
- Plan assets fair value = $275,000
- Net cumulative unrecognized actuarial gains = $15,000

The curtailment event shrinks the present value of the benefit obligation by $20,000, to $280,000. Also, 20% of the net cumulative unrecognized actuarial gains are associated with that portion of the obligation that was eliminated by the curtailment. These alterations are incorporated into the following table:

| | Before Curtailment | Gain on Curtailment | After Curtailment |
|---|---|---|---|
| Present value of obligation | $300,000 | -$20,000 | $280,000 |
| Fair value of plan assets | -275,000 | -- | -275,000 |
| | 25,000 | -20,000 | 5,000 |
| Unrecognized actuarial gains | 15,000 | 3,000 | 18,000 |
| Net liability | $40,000 | -$17,000 | $23,000 |

Based on the preceding "gain on curtailment" information, Armadillo's controller records the following entry to record the gain on curtailment:

| | Debit | Credit |
|---|---|---|
| Accrued pension cost | 17,000 | |
|     Curtailment gain | | 17,000 |

## Termination Benefits

An employer may provide a certain set of benefits to employees that it terminates. Examples of termination benefits are lump-sum cash payments, a series of periodic payments in the future, or a combination of the two. The employer should recognize a liability and expense for the full amount of these benefits as soon as terminated employees accept the termination offer to which the benefits are linked, and the payment amount can be reasonably estimated. This expense should include the amount of any lump-sum payments made, as well as the present value of any future payments to be made. To determine the amount of termination expense to recognize, use the following calculation:

| | |
|---|---|
| + | Actuarial present value of accumulated pension benefits, including termination benefits |
| - | Actuarial present value of accumulated pension benefits, without termination benefits |
| = | Termination benefits to charge to expense |

**Combined Pension Plans**

A company may elect to combine several of its pension plans, which means that the assets of each predecessor plan can now be used to satisfy the obligations of the combined plan. The company should create a single amortization schedule for each of the pension costs that must be amortized. The amortization periods incorporated into these schedules shall be based on a weighted average of the remaining amortization periods used by the individual pension plans before they were combined. However, the prior service cost associated with each individual pension plan shall continue to be amortized under the old amortization schedules formulated prior to the combination of plans.

## Defined Contribution Plans

Under a defined contribution plan, the employer commits to contribute a certain amount to a pension fund in each period, based on a formula that incorporates such factors as the age of each employee, years of service, and employee compensation levels. There is no commitment to pay a specific benefit at a later date – the commitment is only the amount initially paid into the plan. The amount eventually paid to employees is comprised of the original contribution amount, the income generated by the pension fund, and forfeitures of funds by the early termination of employees. This approach massively simplifies the estimation of pension costs.

The accounting for a defined contribution plan is simplicity itself (as opposed to the accounting just described for a defined benefit plan). The employer charges its contributions to expense as incurred. If such a plan calls for additional payments to be made after an employee leaves the company, the estimated cost of these additional payments shall be accrued during the service period of the applicable employee. If the employer does not pay the full amount of its obligation into the pension fund, it reports a liability in this amount on its balance sheet. In those rare cases where the employer pays more than the amount of its obligation into the pension fund, it reports the excess amount as an asset on its balance sheet.

In those cases where an employer terminates a defined benefit plan and shifts the assets in the plan to a defined contribution plan that is a replacement plan, there may be an excess of assets in the replacement plan over the required annual contribution to the plan. If so, the employer should maintain the excess assets in a suspense account until such time as they are needed to fund the replacement account. Until the assets in the suspense account are used to fund the replacement account, the employer continues to retain the risks and rewards of ownership associated with those assets, and so shall account for the assets within its own balance sheet.

## Presentation of Retirement Benefit Information

If an employer has a defined benefit pension or other postretirement plan, it should provide line items in the financial statements for the following information:

- State the service cost component of net periodic pension cost and net periodic postretirement benefit cost in the same line item or items in the income statement as other compensation costs caused by services rendered by employees during the period.[2]
- Separately state the funding status of each plan in the financial statements, including the funding of non-pension postretirement benefit plans.
- Itemize the recognized amounts of related assets, current liabilities, and non-current liabilities.
- Classify any underfunded plan liabilities as being current or noncurrent liabilities, or both. For the purposes of this classification, a current plan liability is the excess amount of the actuarial present value of the longer of the benefits payable in the next 12 months or the operating cycle, over the fair value of plan assets.
- If a plan is overfunded, classify the overfunding as a noncurrent asset.

---

**EXAMPLE**

Atlas Machining Company has a projected benefit obligation of $400,000, and the fair value of its plan assets is $310,000. This means that Atlas' pension plan is underfunded, so it reports a pension liability of $90,000 on its balance sheet, which is the difference between the two figures. If Atlas' plan asset had instead had a fair value of $450,000, it would report a pension asset of $50,000 (calculated as $450,000 plan assets - $400,000 projected benefit obligation).

---

## Retirement Benefit Disclosures

The disclosures related to defined benefit plans vary for publicly-held and privately-held companies, so the requirements are stated separately for each type of business. There is also a discussion of the much more abbreviated disclosures for defined contribution plans.

### Defined Benefit Plan Disclosures for Public Companies

The following disclosures related to retirement benefits are required for a publicly-held business, and are to be provided separately for pension plans and other postretirement plans:

- *Benefit obligation reconciliation.* The beginning and ending balances of the benefit obligation, showing the reconciling effects of service cost, interest

---

[2] Not including the amount of these costs that is being capitalized in connection with the manufacture or construction of an asset, such as inventory or a building.

cost, participant contributions, actuarial gains and losses, exchange rate effects, benefits paid, plan amendments, business combinations, divestitures, curtailments, settlements, and termination benefits.

- *Assets reconciliation.* A reconciliation of the beginning and ending balances of the fair value of plan assets, showing the reconciling effects of the return on plan assets, exchange rate changes, employer contributions, participant contributions, benefits paid, business combinations, divestitures, and settlements.
- *Funded status.* The funded status of each plan, with the related assets, current liabilities, and noncurrent liabilities.
- *Plan asset information.* Investment policies and strategies, target allocation percentages, the fair value of each class of plan assets as of each balance sheet date, the approach used to estimate the long-term rate of return on assets, and enough information for users to assess the inputs and valuation techniques needed to develop fair value measurements (including a discussion of how the fair value hierarchy was used).
- *Accumulated benefit obligation*[3]
- *Benefit payments.* The expected benefits to be paid in each of the next five years, and in aggregate for the five years thereafter.
- *Contributions paid.* The estimated amount of contribution payments expected during the next fiscal year, aggregating required, discretionary, and noncash contributions.
- *Net benefit cost.* The net benefit cost recognized, separately stating the service cost, interest cost, expected return on plan assets, gain or loss, prior service cost, transition asset, and gain or loss caused by settlements or curtailments.
- *Other comprehensive income.* The net gain or loss, the net prior service cost or credit, and reclassification adjustments recognized for the period in other comprehensive income.
- *Accumulated other comprehensive income.* Any amounts in accumulated other comprehensive income that have not been recognized in net periodic benefit cost, along with the net gain or loss, net prior service cost or credit, and net transition asset or obligation.
- *Assumptions.* In tabular format, the assumptions for assumed discount rates, rates of compensation increase, and expected long-term rates of return on plan assets that were used to calculate the benefit obligation and net benefit cost.
- *Cost trends.* The projected trends in health care costs for the next year, as well as the pattern of change thereafter, the ultimate trend rate, and when the ultimate rate is expected.
- *Change effects.* The effect of a one-percent increase and decrease in the health care cost trend rate on service and interest cost components of net periodic postretirement health care benefit costs and the accumulated benefit obligation.

---

[3] The present value of an employee's pension, based on the employee's accumulated work to date.

- *Asset contents.* The types and amounts of securities issued by the employer and related parties that are part of plan assets, significant transactions between the plan and the employer and related parties in the period, and the amount of future annual benefits covered by insurance contracts.
- *Amortization.* The method used to amortize prior service amounts or net gains and losses.
- *Commitments.* Any significant commitment incorporated into the benefit obligation, such as a history of granting benefit increases.
- *Termination benefits.* The cost of providing termination benefits during the period, and the nature of these benefits.
- *Other changes.* The nature of any other significant changes in the benefit obligation or plan assets.
- *Assets returned to employer.* The amount of any plan assets to be returned to the employer in the next year, and the timing of the return.
- *Expected recognition.* The accumulated other comprehensive income amounts to be recognized as part of net periodic benefit cost in the next year, stating the net gain or loss, net prior service cost or credit, and the net transition asset or obligation.

The preceding disclosures should be aggregated for all of an employer's defined benefit pension plans and other postretirement plans, unless stating the disclosures separately for each plan will provide useful information.

---

**EXAMPLE**

Camelot Construction discloses the following information about its retirement plans in the notes accompanying its financial statements:

> The company has a funded defined benefit pension plan that covers substantially all of its employees. The plan provides defined benefits based on years of service and the average salary of employees over their final five years of service.

**Obligations and Funded Status of Pension Benefits**

| (000s) | 20X3 | 20X2 |
|---|---|---|
| Change in benefit obligation: | | |
| Benefit obligation at beginning of year | $2,190 | $2,200 |
| Service cost | 110 | 120 |
| Interest cost | 65 | 50 |
| Amendments | 25 | 10 |
| Actuarial loss | 15 | |
| Benefits paid | -205 | -190 |
| Benefit obligation at end of year | $2,200 | $2,190 |

**Change in Plan Assets**

| (000s) | 20X3 | 20X2 |
|---|---|---|
| Change in plan assets: | | |
| Fair value of plan assets at beginning of year | $1,845 | $1,860 |
| Actual return on plan assets | 65 | 50 |
| Employer contributions | 180 | 125 |
| Benefits paid | -205 | -190 |
| Fair value of plan assets at end of year | $1,885 | $1,845 |
| Funded status at end of year | -$315 | -$345 |

**Components of Net Periodic Benefit Cost and Other Amounts Recognized in Accumulated Other Comprehensive Income**

| (000s) | 20X3 | 20X2 |
|---|---|---|
| Net periodic benefit cost: | | |
| Service cost | $110 | $120 |
| Interest cost | 65 | 50 |
| Expected return on plan assets | 45 | 40 |
| Amortization of prior service cost | 15 | 10 |
| Net periodic benefit cost | $235 | $220 |

**Other Changes in Plan Assets and Benefit Obligations Recognized in Other Comprehensive Income**

| (000s) | 20X3 | 20X2 |
|---|---|---|
| Net loss (gain) | $30 | -$20 |
| Prior service cost | 50 | -- |
| Amortization of prior service cost | -15 | -10 |
| Total recognized in other comprehensive income | 65 | -30 |
| Total recognized in net periodic benefit cost and other comprehensive income | $300 | $190 |

The estimated net loss and prior service cost that will be amortized from accumulated other comprehensive income into net periodic benefit cost over the next fiscal year are $3,000 and $12,000, respectively.

**Weighted-Average Assumptions used to Determine Pension Obligations at December 31**

|  | 20X3 | 20X2 |
|---|---|---|
| Discount rate | 4.50% | 3.75% |
| Rate of compensation increase | 4.25% | 4.00% |

**Weighted-Average Assumptions used to Determine Net Periodic Benefit Cost at December 31**

|  | 20X3 | 20X2 |
|---|---|---|
| Discount rate | 4.75% | 4.00% |
| Expected long-term return on plan assets | 5.50% | 5.00% |
| Rate of compensation increase | 4.75% | 4.25% |

### Plan Assets

The company follows an investment strategy of 60 percent in long-term growth investments and 40 percent in short-term investments from which benefits can be paid. Target allocations are 70 percent in large cap equities and 20 percent in corporate bonds, in all cases with issuers located in the United States and Europe. Ten percent of the target allocation is to other investments approved in advance by the board of directors. The fair value of Camelot's pension plan assets at December 31, 20X3 is as follows:

**Fair Value of Pension Plan Assets**

|  |  | Fair Value Measurements at 12/31/X3 | | |
|---|---|---|---|---|
| (000s) | Total | Quoted Prices in Active Markets for Identical Assets (Level 1) | Significant Observable Inputs (Level 2) | Significant Unobservable Inputs (Level 3) |
| Cash | $90 | $90 | | |
| Equity securities | | | | |
|   U.S. large-cap | 750 | 750 | | |
|   Europe large-cap | 480 | 480 | | |
| Corporate bonds | 375 | | $375 | |
| Hedge funds | 120 | | | $120 |
| Real estate | 70 | | | 70 |
| | $1,885 | $1,320 | $375 | $190 |

The company expects to contribute $200,000 to its pension plan in 20X4.

## Defined Benefit Plan Disclosures for Private Companies

The following disclosures related to retirement benefits are required for a privately-held business:

- *Benefit obligation.* The benefit obligation, funded status, and fair value of plan assets.
- *Contributions.* Employer and participant contributions, and the amount of benefits paid.
- *Plan asset information.* Investment policies and strategies, target allocation percentages, the fair value of each class of plan assets as of each balance sheet date, the approach used to estimate the long-term rate of return on assets assumption, and enough information for users to assess the inputs and valuation techniques used to develop fair value measurements (including a discussion of how the fair value hierarchy was used).
- *Accumulated benefit obligation*
- *Benefit payments.* The expected benefits to be paid in each of the next five years, and in aggregate for the five years thereafter.
- *Contributions paid.* The estimated amount of contribution payments expected during the next fiscal year, aggregating required, discretionary, and noncash contributions.
- *Assets and liabilities.* The postretirement benefit assets, and both current and noncurrent postretirement benefit liabilities.
- *Other comprehensive income.* The net gain or loss, the net prior service cost or credit, and reclassification adjustments recognized for the period in other comprehensive income.
- *Accumulated other comprehensive income.* Any amounts in accumulated other comprehensive income that have not been recognized in net periodic benefit cost, along with the net gain or loss, net prior service cost or credit, and net transition asset or obligation.
- *Assumptions.* In tabular format, the assumptions for assumed discount rates, rates of compensation increase, and expected long-term rates of return on plan assets that were used to calculate the benefit obligation and net benefit cost.
- *Cost trends.* The projected trends in health care costs for the next year, as well as the pattern of change thereafter, the ultimate trend rate, and when the ultimate rate is expected.
- *Asset contents.* The types and amounts of securities issued by the employer and related parties that are part of plan assets, significant transactions between the plan and the employer and related parties in the period, and the amount of future annual benefits covered by insurance contracts.
- *Nonroutine events.* The nature of significant nonroutine events, including divestitures, combinations, amendments, curtailments, and settlements.
- *Recognition of accumulated other comprehensive income.* Any amounts in accumulated other comprehensive income to be recognized in the next year

as net periodic benefit cost, showing the net gain or loss, net prior service cost or credit, and net transition asset or obligation.

- *Assets returned to employer.* The amount of any plan assets to be returned to the employer in the next year, and the timing of the return.
- *Net periodic benefit.* The amount of net periodic benefit cost recognized in the period.

## Disclosures for Defined Benefit Plans in Interim Periods

The disclosures for retirement benefits in interim financial statements are greatly reduced from the requirements to be listed in annual financial statements. Only the following disclosures are required in the interim statements of a publicly-held company:

- *Net benefit cost.* The net benefit cost for the period, separately stating service cost, interest cost, the expected return on plan assets, gain or loss, prior service cost or credit, the transition asset or obligation, and any gains or losses due to a settlement or curtailment.
- *Contributions.* The total contributions paid by the employer, if significantly different from the amount disclosed in the preceding annual financial statements. This disclosure can aggregate noncash and discretionary contributions, as well as contributions required by funding regulations or laws.

---

**EXAMPLE**

Excalibur Shaving Company reports the following components of its net periodic benefit cost:

|  | First Quarter Pension Benefits | First Quarter Other Benefits |
|---|---|---|
| Service cost | $70,000 | $32,000 |
| Interest cost | 84,000 | 46,000 |
| Expected return on plan assets | -53,000 | -12,000 |
| Amortization of prior service cost | 14,000 | -6,000 |
| Amortization of net loss | 4,000 | -- |
| Net periodic benefit cost | $119,000 | $60,000 |

Excalibur also includes the following disclosure in the footnotes accompanying its financial statements:

The Company previously disclosed in its financial statements for the year ended December 31, 20X2 that it expected to contribute $1,000,000 to its pension plan in 20X3. As of March 31, 20X3, $200,000 of contributions have been made. The Company presently anticipates contributing an additional $900,000 to fund its pension plan in 20X3, for a total of $1,100,000.

---

A privately-held company has even fewer required disclosures in an interim period, which are:

- *Contributions.* The total contributions paid by the employer, if significantly different from the amount disclosed in the preceding annual financial statements.

**Disclosures for Defined Contribution Plans**

If a company has one or more defined contribution plans, it should disclose the amount of cost recognized for these plans for all periods presented in the financial statements. These costs should be disclosed separately from the costs disclosed for any defined benefit plans. Also, describe the nature of any significant changes during the presented periods that affect the comparability of the information from period to period. Examples of such comparability events are the effects of an acquisition or divestiture.

## Summary

When a company has a defined benefit plan, the number of variables impacting the amount of future payments makes it extremely difficult to recognize expenses that actually approximate the amounts that are later paid. In many cases, the variance between actual and estimated pension costs can have a profound impact on the financial results reported by a business, to the extent that users of this information may decide that the financial statements cannot be relied upon to reveal the actual results and condition of the business. The result can be additional analysis by investors, who use their own estimates of future pension liabilities to adjust the company's financial statements, and make investment decisions based on their own estimates.

The level of confusion engendered by defined benefit plans bolsters the case for not entering into such plans. As an alternative, the accounting for defined contribution plans is neat, simple, and highly predictable, and results in more reliable financial statements. While the complaints of accountants are hardly likely to convince management to avoid using defined benefit plans, these issues can be considered alongside other factors, such as the massive long-term liabilities associated with defined benefit plans, to reduce their use.

# Glossary

**A**

*Accumulated benefit obligation.* The present value of an employee's pension, based on the employee's accumulated work to date.

*Actuarial present value.* The present value of payments that an entity expects to pay under a retirement benefit plan to its existing and past employees for services already rendered.

*Amortization.* The systematic reduction of a recognized liability by recognizing gains, or by recognizing losses related to an asset.

**D**

*Defined benefit plan.* A retirement benefit plan under which payments to former employees are fixed based on a formula.

*Defined contribution plan.* An arrangement under which a business pays a fixed amount into a benefit plan for employees.

*Discount rate.* A rate used to reflect the time value of money, which is used to determine the present value of future cash flows.

**M**

*Mortality rate.* The number of deaths during a period of time among a group of people.

**N**

*Net periodic pension cost.* The cost of a pension plan for a reporting period, as stated in an employer's financial statements.

*Net periodic postretirement benefit cost.* The cost of a postretirement benefit plan, as stated in an employer's financial statements.

**P**

*Pension benefit.* A payout from a retirement plan to a retired person.

*Plan amendment.* A change to the terms of an existing retirement plan.

*Plan assets.* Those assets that have been set aside to provide for pension benefits.

*Plan curtailment.* A triggering event that reduces the expected years of future service of current employees, or eliminates the accrual of benefits for future employee service.

*Prior service costs.* The cost of benefits retroactively granted in a plan amendment.

*Projected benefit obligation.* The actuarial present value of future benefits attributed to service already rendered by employees.

## U

*Unfunded projected benefit obligation.* When a plan's projected benefit obligation is greater than the fair value of plan assets.

# Index

www.ingramcontent.com/pod-product-compliance
Lightning Source LLC
Chambersburg PA
CBHW081652060726
47593CB00023B/2850